Animals That Help Us

Service Animals

by Alice Boynton

Red Chair Press   Egremont, Massachusetts

Look! Books are produced and published by Red Chair Press:

Red Chair Press LLC   PO Box 333   South Egremont, MA 01258-0333

www.redchairpress.com

Publisher's Cataloging-In-Publication Data

Names: Boynton, Alice Benjamin

Title: Service animals / by Alice Boynton.

Description: Egremont, Massachusetts : Red Chair Press, [2018] | Series: Look! books : Animals that help us | Interest age level: 004-007. | Includes Now You Know fact-boxes, a glossary, and resources for additional reading. | Includes index. | Summary: "You know that pets can be fun. But some dogs, horses, pigs, and more have important jobs to do. With Animals That Help Us young readers will discover how animals help us stay safe. Service animals are uniquely trained to help when someone is not able to help themselves. Readers learn how and why monkeys are some of the most important service animals. Readers meet other service animals such as small horses, dogs, and birds."--Provided by publisher.

Identifiers: ISBN 978-1-63440-318-4 (library hardcover) | ISBN 978-1-63440-366-5 (paperback) | ISBN 978-1-63440-324-5 (ebook)

Subjects: LCSH: Animals as aids for people with disabilities--Juvenile literature. | CYAC: Working animals.

Classification: LCC HV1569.6 .B69 2018 (print) | LCC HV1569.6 (ebook) | DDC 362.40483 [E]--dc23

LCCN 2017947560

Photo credits: Cover: Helping Hands: Monkey Helpers; p 7, 9, 13: Trillium Studios; p. 11: Erica Noyes; p. 5, 22: Courtesy of The Guide Horse Foundation; p 3, 21: © William Thomas Cain/Getty Images; p. 15, 24: iStock; p. 17, 19: © REUTERS/Alamy

Printed in the United States of America

0718 1P CGF18

Table of Contents

Animals at Your Service

Have you ever seen a monkey turn on a light switch? What about a horse on a train? You may say, "No way!" But read on. Find out about these service animals and the important work they do.

5

Monkey Helpers

Some people can't use their arms or legs. Animals like Capuchin (*CAP yoo chin*) monkeys can help them. Why monkeys? Monkeys have hands and fingers like ours.

Good to Know

Capuchins are small, friendly monkeys. They weigh between 3 and 11 pounds. That's comfortable for your lap!

Monkeys can turn lights and TVs on and off. They can put a DVD in a player. *Oops*— a cell phone falls down. A monkey can pick it up. And what if someone has an annoying itch? A monkey uses a soft cloth to scratch it. Very handy!

But a monkey has to learn to do these things. How? It goes to monkey school. Monkeys are very **intelligent**. A trainer shows the monkey each skill. The monkey copies what the trainer does. *It's monkey see, monkey do!*

11

After training, the monkey can do many helpful tasks. It can fetch a bottle and unscrew the top. Then it can put in a straw. Awesome! The monkey is ready to be a good helper. But it will have time to monkey around, too!

The monkey and its partner will be best friends for life.

Hearing Dogs

Technology helps deaf people. Hearing aids make sounds louder. A doorbell sets off flashing lights. An alarm clock makes the bed pillow shake. But some deaf people also have dogs to help them.

Good to Know

A deaf person is someone who cannot hear.

The dog's touch means, *I hear something. Follow me.*

15

The hearing dogs are trained to listen for different sounds. *BZZZZZ!* The dog hears the alarm clock. It nudges the sleeping person. *Time to get up!*

Good to Know

A service dog is almost always working. Even when resting, the dog stays alert for what its person may need.

A trained hearing dog can alert its partner to a

- smoke alarm
- phone
- doorbell
- microwave beeping
- thing that falls, like keys
- baby crying

On the street, the
dog gives signals, too.
It may hear a siren.
The dog's ears perk up.
It looks down the street.
Something's coming! Wait!
The deaf person looks.
Thanks for the warning!

Dogs can hear things before people can see them.

19

Guide Horses

You have probably seen guide dogs for the blind, or people who cannot see. But what about guide horses? Some blind people have **miniature** horses to help them get around.

Good to Know

Miniature horses have hair, not fur. So people who are allergic to the fur on dogs can use the horses.

An animal wearing a vest is working, so do not pet it.

21

A guide horse sleeps in a shed. But it is **housebroken**, so it can be in the house, too. When work is done, it can relax. A snack in the kitchen or a nap on the rug is just right!

The Guide Horse Foundation trains and gives guide horses to the blind at no cost.

Words to Keep

allergic: react by itching or sneezing, for example
housebroken: trained to be indoors
intelligent: smart
miniature: small
technology: a science of new things

Learn More at the Library

Books (Check out these books to learn more.)

A Place for Grace by Jean Davies Okimoto. Sasquatch Books, 1993.

Panda, A Guide Horse for Ann by Rosanna Hansen.
Boyds Mills Press, 2005.

Raising a Hero (A Work for Biscuits Book) by Laura Numeroff.
Cleverkick, 2016.

Web Sites (Ask an adult to show you these web sites.)

Helping Hands Monkey Helpers
https://monkeyhelpers.org

Monkey College (Helping Hands video)
https://www.youtube.com/watch?v=jo4g2aKscaQ

Tonka's Job: Guide Horse (YouTube)
https://www.youtube.com/watch?v=TR9tmRNUBDo

Index

About the Author

Alice Boynton has over 20 years of experience in the classroom. She has written many books on how to teach with nonfiction.